The Power of Mentorship

Emma's Gift: Claire's Journey of Self-Discovery

Judy Robinson

About the Author

I grew up as the third of four sisters in Washington state. Like many, I feared being vulnerable and seen as weak. Yet, it is in those moments of vulnerability and discomfort that we experience the most growth.

I loved my teenage years—friendships, family, school, playing softball—but I always felt like something was missing. I longed for deep communication, to be seen, heard, and understood.

In our family, communication was often superficial: "What's for dinner? How 'about them' Seahawks? What time is the softball game?" I yearned for something more profound, someone special to discuss the deeper aspects of life—navigating life after high school, relationships, the universe, and God.

I hope this book helps you to not fear the 'hard stuff' in life but to welcome and embrace it as a chance to broaden your perspectives and grow as a person. I also hope it encourages you to use your voice, express your thoughts, speak up for yourself, and stay true to your own truth—because only you truly know what that is.

Dedication

This book is dedicated to my daughter, Olivia, and to Dan, who has brought a new light into my life. Olivia, your voice has the power to inspire others and create lasting change, and that is something money can't buy. I want her to know that there is no other voice like hers. The impact you have can last for many years and touch countless lives—not everyone gets that chance.

Dan, you have shown me the beauty of love and partnership in a new chapter of my life. Your support and companionship have been a beacon of hope and joy. Together, you both remind me of the importance of love, growth, and embracing the journey of life.

When was the last time your heart smiled? Your voice can help you share your thoughts and opinions, and it can profoundly impact others. By influencing others, you help them build confidence and take positive action. Your voice is a gift that can inspire others, and that impact will echo for many years.

Acknowledgment

Thank you to my daughter for inspiring me to write about living without fear and discovering who you are and what you have to say in this world.

Knowing yourself, understanding your beliefs, and having the courage to speak up when it matters requires strength, courage, and a deep dive into your heart, soul, and mind for guidance.

Contents

Chapter 1: Identifying Struggles

I have not felt confident or comfortable in my own skin for as long as I can remember. I avoid associating with people because I always regret how I interact with them.

However, living in a world full of people, it is almost impossible to avoid interacting with others. Most importantly, it must not be avoided because it helps you learn about yourself and others over time. It is necessary to speak and communicate your thoughts and opinions to the people in your life so they hear, see, and understand you!

I, Claire, have struggled to voice my opinion from a young age. Belonging to a somewhat conventional family, I have been the quietest of the kids. We are three siblings, among which I am the middle child. My oldest sister, Eve, has been the favorite child in the family. The youngest one, Abby, is the most confident child and a favorite as well.

Being the shy and introverted child in the family, I have always faced difficulties expressing what I needed, wanted, or even thought.

My parents love all of their children dearly, but since I was not so expressive, I faced bias and prejudice, even in the slightest or pettiest of things.

Like I said, my parents have their favorite kid. But you know what? I was never their favorite kid. I never paid attention to it and remained unbothered to an extent, but somewhere in my subconscious, I was affected by the favoritism running in my family. I knew I needed to use my voice and speak my mind, but I didn't quite know how.

Being a simple and uncomplicated child from a very young age, nobody was particularly interested in me. Never did I make trouble or bother my parents. I always helped my siblings and sometimes would face the music for their wrongdoings.

I was one of the brightest kids in my school and always did well. I was somewhat bullied though. Other kids called me a nerd, making fun of how plain I dressed and how studious I was. However, never paying much attention to criticism, I carried on with what I had to do.

But I guess by staying silent and ignoring everything, I showcased myself as a coward, even though I knew I wasn't one. My brain just processed in a way that asked me to avoid any troubling situation or ignore anything that affected me emotionally.

It was a bright Monday morning. I had a science quiz that day, which I had studied thoroughly for. I believed in my abilities, and I was sure that I knew the answers to every possible question the teacher could ask us.

It was 8:00 a.m., and I entered the classroom, ready for the quiz. Everyone settled down at their desks as soon as the bell rang. Ms. Reid, our science teacher, entered the classroom and tidied her desk.

Picking up a piece of chalk from the desk, Ms. Reid wrote the word *QUIZ* on the board in block letters. Every student knew it was time to begin. I was pumped up inside, knowing I had prepared well for the quiz.

Ms. Reid announced, "Let's start."

She asked the first question, "What is the building block of the human body?"

After hearing this question, many students raised their hands to answer. I also raised my hand, hoping Ms. Reid would notice me, but to my dismay, another kid answered the question correctly.

Now everyone was ready for the second question.

Ms. Reid asked, "How many chambers are there in the human heart?"

I knew! I knew the answer to this question, but I didn't raise my hand this time. I wasn't sure if I should answer the question or just sit silently in the classroom hoping nobody would notice me.

Many questions were asked one after another, and now the quiz was about to end. I sat in the corner trying to disappear because I had lost my confidence by then. The problem was not that I didn't know the answer, instead, it was about speaking in front of an audience.

Yes… public speaking! I feared it even if I was confident about my research and knowledge. In the end, the knowledge and research didn't help; I just sat in silence, doubting my abilities in the classroom. Soon the quiz ended and the bell rang. We all left the classroom, and Ms. Reid was alone gathering her stuff from the desk.

Walking out of the classroom, I kept regretting what I had done. I wished I had answered at least one of the many questions and proved myself.

Everyone went their own way, and I went out of the corridor to sit in the garden. I sat down on a bench in the extreme corner of the garden. While sitting there, I could see kids playing basketball. It was one of my favorite sports, and I loved playing it. I was a member of our girls' basketball team at school. I was fit and in good shape. I was tall enough to make a basket and would do it often when I played alone on the basketball court.

The same day in the afternoon, our team had a basketball game with another school. I was prepared for it. My excitement was increasing as the clock ticked. However, I knew that my coach didn't like me much — and I knew why.

It wasn't due to my lack of skills, but he had a favorite on the team, his niece, Bethany. Bethany was the team captain, and the coach, Shane, replaced me from the three-point shooter position with Bethany. Everyone knew that Bethany wasn't as skilled as I was, but nobody spoke about it, including myself. After it happened, I wanted to confront the coach, but I wasn't courageous enough to do it.

I was disappointed in myself for not voicing my opinion; I suffered silently. I was scared of rejection and being misunderstood. Soon the clock ticked 12:00, and everyone gathered on the basketball court, dressed in red jerseys and shorts, all geared up for the game.

Shane, our coach, came and briefed us about the game. I knew he would do the same to me today, what he does every time. He instructed me to pass the ball to Bethany for a three-pointer. But today, I had decided that I would speak up.

The game started, and everyone played skillfully. It continued for a good thirty minutes when the moment came. The three-point shot!

As the moment arrived, my coach started shouting to pass the ball to Bethany from the corner. I stopped for a few seconds, contemplating whether to shoot it myself or pass it to Bethany.

Standing there with the ball in my hand, I glanced at Bethany for a second and then at my coach. I wanted to shoot it myself, but my subconscious betrayed me again.

Hearing my couch screaming from the corner, I felt helpless and passed the ball to Bethany. Our team won the match, and all praises were for Bethany.

Feeling pathetic about myself, I left the basketball court and went to the locker room to change. I stood in front of the bathroom mirror, staring at myself and trying to figure out what was wrong with me. I stared expressionless at myself in the mirror. I knew deep down that I had so much to say, but I was scared to express myself and look like a fool in front of my teammates.

Once again, ignoring everything, I changed my clothes and left the bathroom. As I turned left, exiting the bathroom, I spotted one of my classmates standing between a bunch of school bullies. Glancing at those girls' faces, I immediately recognized that they were our school's famous bullies.

I could see that something wrong was going on there. My friend was stressed, and I could clearly tell from her face.

For an instant, I thought to help her out. After taking a few steps closer to them, I froze for a while, unable to move. Those spiteful bullies were making fun of my friend's clothes and hair.

Looking at the distressful situation in front of me, I lost my confidence altogether. I walked away, trying to ignore what was happening right in front of me.

As I walked past the bullies, I avoided eye contact with my classmates because I had acted like a coward. I knew that I shouldn't have done that and should have stood up for her, knowing that we could've fought against the bullies and given them a taste of their own medicine. However, I still chose to walk away from the situation. I entered my classroom and sat there alone trying to comprehend what I had just done.

The bell for the next period rang, and soon the class became full of students. As I was surrounded by people, I was able to distract myself from my intrusive thoughts. It was the last class of the day. My English instructor came and conducted the class. While the class was going on, I was preoccupied with my thoughts. Physically, I was present there, but mentally, I was still in the hallway of my school, still caught up in the moment when the bullies had surrounded my classmate.

I should have stood up for her and asked them to stop. She wouldn't have been in such a situation if I had intervened. However, none of that happened. What I did was walk away, abstaining from eye contact, and trying my best to ignore everything and just disappear.

I felt guilty… extremely guilty!

Shortly after the class ended, I left the classroom and went to look for my bus. As soon as I spotted it, I got in and sat in my usual spot.

All the way to my home, I kept thinking about what happened that day. I just couldn't get it out of my head. I was trying to look for answers for my lack of self-confidence to stand up for my friend. Analyzing myself, I soon got the answer to it. I guess it was in my subconscious waiting for me to acknowledge it.

I realized what the answer was… I knew that it was because of social media.

Social media helps people in many ways, but for me it turned the situation against me. It made me lose my self-confidence. At one time, I used to be addicted to social media. Watching people my age excel in their lives, thriving, winning competitions, going on vacations, and living the life I had always dreamt of made me think less worthy of myself.

It made me realize that my life was lackluster, uninteresting, and monotonous. I compelled myself to think that the life I had was just downright boring.

I forgot to look at the positive aspects of my life. I failed to understand that a lot of social media is fake and it is based on the amount of likes and followers you have. We choose to show the world tidbits of our lives when we look good and do something fun or cool. It is not a representation of our entire life. People show a few pictures of their cute, perfect relationship, or a trip to Hawaii, but it is just a few pictures. It is not their entire life.

Additionally, I failed to understand myself. Never analyzing the worthy parts of my life and myself, I only focused on the negative ones, and it only got worse when I looked at social media.

I realized how unfair I was to myself and got stuck in a dark place, and finding a way out of it seemed too difficult. Completely lost in my thoughts, and oblivious to my surroundings, I didn't realize that I was just a block away from my home. In a few seconds, I reached my destination and walked off the bus.

Going straight to my room, I placed my bag on the corner table and crawled into bed. I was very tired. I felt physically and mentally drained from my exhausting day and just wanted to nap. I fell asleep as soon as my head hit the pillow and forgot everything that happened that day. I woke up after two hours, freshened up, and completed the homework that my English teacher assigned.

After a short while, I looked at the clock and realized it was already time for dinner. Putting my assignment in my bag, I went down the stairs where my Mom and Dad were busy cooking dinner. My Mom was setting the table and looking at me with a warm smile. Smiling back at her, I settled down on the dining chair.

I was famished. My mother placed the grilled chicken dish with baked potatoes on the table, and everyone in my family settled down to have dinner together. Everyone began eating, and I was again immersed in my thoughts.

I wanted to enjoy dinner, but my brain replayed the day's activities and ruined it. The cycle continued, and I felt pathetic. I still couldn't believe the way I had behaved today. My mind kept replaying what happened throughout the day, making me wonder how to express myself in a healthy way.

Recalling the basketball match, I regretted passing the ball to Bethany. Being the most athletic and fittest in my family, I could have shot the ball and scored, and then all the praise could have been for me, but my lack of courage and self-confidence didn't let that happen.

Pitying myself, I continued eating with my family. I couldn't enjoy it though. The weight in my gut was too much to bear. When I was done with dinner, I helped clean up and went to my room. It was 10:00 p.m., and I felt dizzy and exhausted from the day's events. Wanting to sleep right away, I brushed my teeth first, then went to bed after changing into my pajamas.

I woke up the next morning, got ready for school, and waited for my bus to arrive.

Walking through the hallway to my class, I noticed one of my classmates talking to the bullies from the previous day. Her name was Emma. She lit up the dim hallway with her confidence and inner strength.

Every day I would notice her, admiring her self-confidence and hoping to be like her one day.

I stopped in the hallway for a while, trying to listen to what she was saying to the bullies.

I got a hint of what they were talking about. She confronted the bullies for their pathetic behavior yesterday, and that made me realize how courageous she was.

She stood up for her friend and threatened the bullies!

After witnessing this moment in the hallway, I went to my class and settled down at my desk. It was Ms. Reid's class, and while everyone waited for her to conduct it, I sat there thinking about Emma.

I was awestruck and totally impressed by her. At that moment, I wished to befriend her. I wanted her to mentor me on how to become self-confident.

I attended Ms. Reid's class while thinking about how to talk with Emma. I hoped to talk briefly with her after class, but I was excited and nervous. I felt uncomfortable thinking about it, but something inside urged me to reach out to her.

Chapter 2: Seeking Confidence

Shortly after Ms. Reid's class was concluded, I gathered a bit of courage to approach Emma. Knowing that it wasn't easy for me, I thought profusely about it before giving it a shot. However, before even approaching her, my self-confidence shattered, so I aborted the mission.

I was intimidated by her. The personality and self-confidence she possessed were what I lacked but desired. At the core of my heart, I wanted to become like her. The way she portrayed confidence, bravery, composure, and assertiveness captivated me and inspired me to instill the same qualities in myself.

I couldn't talk to her that day. Watching her standing in the hall after class, I tried to summon the courage to speak to her, but I failed miserably.

It was time to go home already. Coming back home in a depressive state, I walked directly to my room, trying to avoid any interactions with my family. As I lay in my bed, I couldn't stop thinking about the whole scenario that happened to me today in school. My mind was intertwined with thoughts that refused to disappear.

The constant contemplation and preoccupying thoughts coiled my mind, twisting and turning inside and making it nearly impossible to divert my attention to anything else. I had several thoughts and ideas residing in my brain. I adored Emma's personality and truly wanted to be like her—self-confident and self-assured—not afraid to stand up for herself or others. I was scared she would think I was a big dork and reject my request to be my mentor. I had a lot of doubts and concerns about myself.

Crashed down on the bed and looking up at the ceiling pointlessly, I had a revelation that flickered in my mind and made me decide what to do before approaching Emma. I decided to do my own research before speaking to her.

In that very instant, I jumped with excitement and sat straight up on my bed. Pulling out my phone from the pocket of my jeans, I went to Google and typed in *How to find the right mentor.* I pressed the search button, hoping to find some great results. I kept my fingers crossed as my heart pounded in my chest. I was making headway.

To my surprise, I got some great insights regarding my query. Sifting through the results, I clearly understood what basic features and qualities I should look for in a mentor.

A mentor should be someone older than you. Being a little bit older, a mentor can provide you with various insights and wisdom on their life experiences. A mentor should be a trusted advisor, provide guidance, and have a strong perception of various matters, the capacity to engage in different perspectives and opinions, and the ability to mold them accordingly, if need be.

Life is a cycle of constant learning and growth, so sticking to one's own beliefs and not allowing oneself to evolve and learn with time doesn't align with the qualities of a mentor.

I learned that a mentor should be trustworthy, one you can trust and confide in. A mentor should have experience in various aspects of life.

They should be confident and brave, willing to teach others to progress in life, overcome their shortcomings, and set goals for themselves. In other words, they should be emotionally supportive humans and role models.

A little research on the internet helped me gain abundant knowledge about my concern and understand it.

Furthermore, my curiosity made me dive deeper into the topic. As I went into the depths of my research, I looked out for what it means to be a mentor.

It surprised me how important a mentor could be in one's life because they provide guidance, advice, and support to the mentee. Fundamentally, a mentor is a counselor. They share their knowledge based on their experiences in personal or professional life.

A mentor serves as a role model, providing encouragement, constructive feedback, and perspective to help the mentee navigate the challenges of life and make informed decisions.

You can discuss tough subjects with a mentor, such as those about God, the Universe, dating, the afterlife, high school, college, or your career path. They might not give you an absolute answer, but they will encourage and help you. It is more important that they listen well and are supportive. They should be someone who not only has the right tools, but also utilizes what they teach in their own life. Reflecting on their past experiences, a mentor helps a mentee sustain themselves in life, making it better for them in every possible way they can.

By providing feedback to the mentees about their life decisions, choices, perspectives, opinions, and thought processes, a mentor enables them to become a better version of themselves.

Additionally, a mentor's feedback and assistance can be a great help to you. They make a great difference in your life by extending support and helping you in any way they possibly can.

A mentor could be a teacher, a role model, a counselor, an advisor, a sponsor, an advocate, or an ally. Depending solely on the mentee, a mentor could be anyone to whom you relate and look up to for guidance. Continuing with my research, I learned that a mentor is the one who provides you with all the tools to become a better version of yourself.

A ray of hope emerged in my heart after reading about a mentor. Scrutinizing myself, I knew that I severely needed one. I was certain that I could improve my personality if I had a mentor, so I looked forward to getting one, and I hoped that Emma would be the one for me.

Pick Someone Who Shares Your Values

Looking ahead, I knew that knowing what specific qualities I had to look for in my mentor was essential. After careful research, I became aware of picking a mentor who shares my core values with me.

Having a shared set of values helps ensure that the mentor and the mentee work toward the same goals and understand each other's perspectives, therefore you would find their opinions and advice relatable. Being able to resonate with them could bring new perspectives and objectives out of you, making you modify your outlook on life in general.

Pick Someone Who Has The Same Viewpoint of Success

Secondly, it is necessary to look for someone with the same definition of success as you. A mentor should be someone who helps you get to know yourself, what is important to you in your life, what makes you happy, and what you are passionate about. They are someone who can help you bring out the 'real' you, unencumbered by the noise and distractions in life.

Pick Someone Who Has The Same Objectives As You

Your mentor and you should have great communication skills so they can understand your short-term and long-term goals and work with you to help you achieve them.

Pick Someone Who Knows How To Build Relationships

Moreover, a mentor should be confident and have the time and capacity to make and build new professional and/or personal relationships. Building new relationships helps you to grow and think beyond your perceptions. You tend to think outside the box when you meet people with various thought processes, opinions, and beliefs. Eventually, it helps you to grow and broaden your network in terms of professional and personal progress simultaneously.

Pick Someone Willing To Accept Challenges

Furthermore, a mentor should have a challenging approach. Tying your hands, taking a back seat, and sitting in your comfort zone won't lead you to personal growth and development. A challenging mindset that is willing to accept difficult situations and adversities tends to help you grow and flourish. You should search for this quality in your mentor so you will be able to welcome life's challenges and not resist being uncomfortable and doing things out of your comfort zone, enabling you to grow.

Pick Someone Approachable

In conclusion, when you are sure someone has all the qualities your mentor should have, approach them and meet them. Express yourself and ask them to become your mentor. The person who is right for you won't reject this opportunity.

I was so engaged in my research that I forgot about dinner. I put my phone down, got up from my bed, and freshened up. Realizing that I hadn't changed after coming back from school, I quickly took a set of fresh pajamas from my drawer and changed into them. I went down the stairs to the kitchen where my mom stood doing the dishes and she asked, "Where have you been, honey? We were waiting for you at dinner."

"I dozed off for a while," I said. I didn't tell her the real reason why I wasn't there for dinner; I didn't realize what time it was until I was done with my research. I didn't want to share it with anybody right then.

I fixed myself a plate of grilled chicken and mashed potatoes and settled down at the dining table to eat in solace. Shortly after, my mother left the kitchen, and I was there sitting alone, eating my dinner, preoccupied with my thoughts.

I kept thinking about Emma. I tried to figure out if she was the right mentor for me. Analyzing what I learned online, I was sure she would be the right person to be my counselor. She was a couple of years older than me, so she had more experience in life than I had. She was in the same school as me, which was a plus. Observing her from afar, I knew that she was strong and courageous and would accept any challenges that would come her way. In addition to that, she was confident enough to make and build new relationships with people, whereas I felt totally inadequate in that department. She also seemed courageous and possessed a strong and assertive personality.

I finished my meal, washed my plate, and went to my room. It was time to sleep, and I felt exhausted. I dozed off as soon as I put my head on the pillow. The next morning, I woke up with a fresh mindset. I was certain that I was going to ask Emma to be my mentor. I had a little spark in myself, wishing that things would turn for me. I wanted to change myself, the way I think and the way I behave.

Immediately, I got up from the bed and went to change. Within a few minutes, I got ready for school and went down where my mother was waiting for me at the breakfast table. I was in a hurry to reach school.

"Why are you in such a hurry, Claire? Come here, sit, and have your breakfast first," she said.

I slowed down and turned to the dining table. I sat down and quickly gulped down my breakfast as fast as I could. I could feel a tingle of nervousness in my hands and mind because today was the day when I was going to ask Emma directly.

"Thanks, Mom. I love you! Bye!" I said, and walked out of the front door.

"I love you too, honey," my mother responded.

My bus arrived as soon as I reached the bus stop. I climbed onto the bus and took the front spot.

On my way to school, I kept thinking about how I would ask Emma the question I eagerly wanted to ask.

I thought to myself that no matter what happened today, I had to approach her. I tried my best to pump myself up.

After fifteen minutes, the bus dropped us at school. I headed down the bus stairs and went straight to the hallway to look for Emma. It was only 7:30 a.m., and class didn't start until 8:00 a.m.

Far away in the hallway, I spotted her. She stood tall and strong in her grandeur and outshined everyone around her. I kept my composure and proceeded to walk towards her.

Walking through the hallway felt so difficult that it took ten minutes to cross through. My legs were weak and wobbly, and I could feel my heart pounding in my chest.

I was extremely nervous and felt like I was about to collapse. I was worried that she wouldn't agree to it and make fun of me. What if she thought that I was a stupid dork?

All these questions and thoughts arose in my mind as I walked toward Emma, but I managed to compose myself and made it through the hallway.

She stood facing her locker, busy arranging her books. I waited for her to turn around. The next minute, she closed her locker and locked it.

As she turned around. I greeted her with a smile. "Hi, Emma. I'm Claire. How are you?"

For a second, she looked confused, but she responded to me in the sweetest way possible.

"Hey, Claire. I'm good. Thank you. How are you?" she answered.

As the ice-breaking session commenced, I felt relief accumulating inside me. I wasn't as nervous as I was before then.

"I am good, Emma."

"If you are not busy doing anything important, can I talk to you for a while?" I asked her, hoping for a positive response.

"Yes, sure. Is this something about class?" She asked.

Her tone and body language made me calm down instantly. She was kind and welcoming, and I felt comfortable and at ease.

"Yeah… kind of. I want to tell you everything in detail. If you don't mind…" I said hesitantly.

"Oh, yes, sure! We can sit outside and talk about anything you want to," she said with a reassuring tone.

I was surprised by the warmth and concern she had in her voice. It was refreshing for me how empathic and kind-hearted she was.

Emma and I went straight to the courtyard and sat at the small table by one of the trees.

I gathered up my courage and told her everything about myself. I told her how I struggled with my self-esteem and how I lacked confidence. Besides that, I shared everything that I struggled with in school and at home.

She was all ears and listened to me with complete attention.

After I was done talking, then it was time to ask the main question.

"Will you become my mentor?" I asked her, with a hint of nervousness in my tone. "I really admire your personality, and I wish to be like you. I like how confident and strong you are, how you voice your opinion and speak up for others, and how confidently you walk through the hallway and into the classroom. I want to be just like you!" I expressed what I had on my mind, and I eagerly waited for her response.

Emma looked at me with a subtle expression of surprise on her face. She smiled shyly and said, "Thank you very much for your appreciation, Claire. I am grateful you think so highly of me."

She paused for a second, and I thought she would decline my request. My heart was pounding, and my hands were sweaty.

She continued, "Yes, sure! I would love to be your mentor."

I was delighted and relieved!

"I will help advise and guide you the best I can. You can ask me about anything you want to," she added. Emma grabbed my hand and gave me a gentle squeeze.

I was so happy. A spark in my heart emerged, making me believe I could improve now. I hoped that I would regain my confidence.

It was almost 8:00 a.m., and it was time for our class. Our meeting ended on a good note, and we went to the class together, making small talk along the way.

Chapter 3: Social Media Cleanse - Watering the Seed of Inner Beauty

Emma and I walked through the hallway and reached our classroom. We went to our designated desks and settled down, as it was time for our teacher to arrive soon.

As everyone waited for Ms. Reid, I sat there feeling relieved.

"Oh God, it seems like a huge burden was taken off my chest!" I murmured to myself and let out a sigh.

It felt like I had found a confidant, a friend that I never had before. Someone I could confide in and share my thoughts, insecurities, and vulnerabilities with.

Something changed the moment I came into the classroom with Emma. I found myself a bit more confident than before. I had a bit of self-reassurance because I had a friend now, a mentor, and a confidant, someone on my side.

The hope for freedom from my intrusive thoughts began. I was beginning to trust myself and feel empowered.

Soon Ms. Reid entered the classroom to conduct the lecture for the day. I was physically present in the classroom, but mentally, I was a million miles away.

With the blink of an eye, the class was adjourned. Everyone picked up their bags and books and left the classroom immediately, while I sat over there contemplating and watching everyone leave as they passed by me.

A voice behind me caught my attention.

"Hey… what's up? Are you okay?"

There she was… my mentor. I thought to myself.

Emma came near my desk and sat in front of me. She could sense that something didn't seem quite right with me.

I responded, "Yeah, I am fine."

She said, "But you don't look fine."

I looked at her in silence, deciding whether I should tell her my vulnerabilities and my insecurities or not.

The next second she said, "You can tell me if something is wrong."

Pausing for a couple of seconds in-between, she continued to say jokingly, "After all, I am your mentor."

As she said this, she chuckled, and I laughed along with her.

Self-doubt and lack of confidence made me ponder over my decision for a brief while. I wondered if I should tell her what was bothering me or give some time for our newly-built bond to grow and strengthen a bit more.

While I was preoccupied with my thoughts, Emma sat there patiently, examining my face and trying to comprehend what was happening inside my mind. I clenched my fists because of extreme nervousness, while signs of confusion and vulnerability were evident on my face. I was dying of shame and self-doubt. I wanted to run far away and hide from everyone.

Emma snapped her fingers in front of me with a soft, reassuring smile on her face. I instantly traveled back to my conscious self from being lost in my thoughts.

"Do you want to talk about it, whatever you are thinking about?" she asked.

Finally, I gathered the courage to speak and replied shyly, "Yeah… I want to talk about it, but I am unsure if I should tell you my insecurities immediately."

Emma, being her confident self, replied, "It's okay. We can talk whenever you want to talk about it,"

"Don't you have to attend your basketball practice today?" She added.

I totally forgot that I had basketball practice today.

"Oh, yes! I forgot. Thanks for reminding me." I said, as I hurriedly got up from my desk and started gathering up my things.

"Do you want to join me?" I asked Emma.

"Yes, sure!" She said.

Both of us exited the classroom and walked toward the court.

What a surreal feeling it was to be walking with my newfound friend in the hallway. I had never had real friends, and now it felt different. As I walked with Emma toward the court, I mentioned, "I have to tell you something important that has been bothering me for a long time, and it has shattered my self-confidence. Would you be interested in listening to me?"

Emma responded immediately, "I will listen to you, Claire. You are my friend, and I will be all ears whenever you want to speak to me."

We reached the basketball court, and I immediately went to the locker room. Emma went to the bleachers to watch me practice.

After forty-five minutes my practice ended, and I joined Emma at the bleachers.

"Wow, you are such a good player," she remarked.

I was on cloud nine after hearing such inspiring words from someone I considered my friend and mentor.

"Thank you," I responded.

Emma waited for me as I changed clothes. It was time to go home now, so we walked together to our designated buses to go home.

I was exhausted from the practice session, so I dozed off as soon as I got home. After waking up from a nap, I felt fresh and energetic.

Something felt different that day. I was in a better mood. I went to grab something to eat from the kitchen. I ate dinner and sat down with my family for a while. Everyone was watching a new television show which I wasn't interested in. I was lost in my thoughts of the events earlier in the day.

After an hour, I went back to my room. I laid down on my bed and contemplated talking to Emma about how I feel about myself whenever I go on social media.

I was certain that something was wrong with me, and this behavior of mine wasn't normal.

I was going to discuss my concerns with Emma tomorrow and eagerly looked forward to her response.

It was a bright, sunny day, and I looked forward to our talk with a fresh sense of excitement. I waited for Emma in the hallway.

She was walking toward the building, and I spotted her from afar.

We greeted each other warmly and proceeded to our first class of the day. After attending the class, we went to the cafeteria and sat at a table in the corner.

"I want to talk to you about something important that has been bothering me for a long time," I said.

Emma looked at me carefully.

"I feel inferior whenever I look at someone on social media… let me show you a post," I added hesitantly.

I showed Emma a Facebook post from one of our classmates. She posted a picture of her and her date, ready for the homecoming dance. She was wearing a super-cute outfit and flaunted her new haircut. She looked beautiful, and her date was the quarterback on the football team.

I felt so inadequate about myself when I saw her. I wanted to look pretty like she did in that cute new outfit.

"I feel like I need to lose weight, get a new hairstyle, and find a date for the prom. I am so plain Jane."

I stopped after explaining to her everything that I felt.

Emma listened to me carefully and didn't say anything for a minute. I guess she was contemplating what to say about my feelings and how to respond.

"It is okay to feel this way, but your self-worth shouldn't be based on a hairstyle or an outfit," she said.

I was amazed to hear her response. Maybe I was expecting something else. I was scared that she would judge me, but to my surprise, she had a very positive response.

"Trust me, all these things don't matter that much. You are so much more than what you look like on the outside. Your real beauty lies beneath it. That is where you will find your true beauty, and it is not up for negotiation." Emma said.

We had a detailed conversation about the topic. The way she explained everything to me started to make a lot of sense.

She made me realize that I shouldn't be bothered by the appearance of others or myself. How cute or fashionable someone dresses doesn't have anything to do with their worth. Teenagers get intimidated by stupid stuff quite often.

They tend to put excessive pressure on trivial things that don't have a lot of significance in life.

We often analyze our worth based on our exterior, but we should be focusing and working more on our interior, our unique abilities, and our potential.

I pondered over it after Emma stopped talking. I guess she was right.

I had done the same with myself. Every time I went on social media, I felt small and insignificant. I was attracted to all the insignificant and petty things, but I realized I was being unfair to myself.

Emma made everything clear to me. I was impressed by how insightful and smart she was.

I was astonished by how she knew her worth; contrary to it, I was completely unaware of my own.

I asked her, "How should I become aware of my self-worth?"

"Look beyond the material things and analyze your inner self. You are so much more than your face and body. When you focus your energy on serving and giving of yourself to others, rather than being worried about your appearance, that is where your real beauty lies." Emma said.

I listened to her carefully.

She made me understand how we should focus on our inner self rather than our outward appearance only. We should focus on how kind, compassionate, empathetic, and affectionate we are. The focus should be on our values, integrity, kindness, and honesty.

Emma validated my feelings and told me it's normal to compare yourself with others, especially teenagers. Your real beauty is an inside job, self-development from the inside out.

Teenagers think that if they get a new hairstyle, wear the right makeup, or have a football quarterback for a boyfriend, it will make them feel better. Actually, it works the opposite way, which is that you need to work on yourself: be your own best friend, be kind to yourself, focus on other people, and help others, rather than worrying about yourself and what other people think of you. The truth is that most people are worried about what others think of them. So, the best thing to do is just be your authentic self and don't worry about what others think of you.

Your 'true' beauty comes from what you have built and created on the inside, not your hairstyle, the brand of your shoes, or the type of jeans you wear.

"But how do I work on my self-worth? I just can't seem to do it," I asked Emma.

"It is not impossible. You just have to focus on your ambition, what you are good at, what makes you happy, and make a plan to reach your goal."

"I don't know how to do it," I said.

"It's okay. Let me guide you."

"I would suggest you restrict your usage of social media for a while because you have analyzed that it makes you question your self-worth. Give yourself a break, and go on a social media cleanse." Emma spoke calmly.

She explained how I could do it.

She convinced me to stop using social media for a while and focus on bettering myself.

I got the point and knew what I had to do. I decided to turn things around for myself. I decided I would focus on being a good person.

I decided to work on my internal growth, progress, and self-development. Self-confidence and self-worth were my new mottos. I wanted to focus on my inner beauty rather than outward appearance. I knew that I wanted to thrive.

I understood my self-worth and decided to stop using all social media platforms until I worked on improving myself and progressing. Emma helped me realize what I lacked and what made me feel this way.

The best thing I had done in a while was gather enough self-confidence to approach Emma and ask her to be my mentor, and not just that, but I also found a friend in her. She helped me focus on what really matters, which is internal growth and self-development.

Thankfully, I had decided to work on my self-development, and I looked forward to it.

Chapter 4: Journey to Self-Awareness

Emma suggested taking it slow.

After she taught me how to analyze my self-worth, she told me about self-awareness. At first, I had no clue about its importance, but she assured me that by the end of this lesson, I would know a lot about it.

I was ready to learn to become self-aware and to understand myself better. Knowing my self-worth and self-awareness might correlate and would be equally important to enhance my personality, I looked forward to the lesson enthusiastically.

The next day after class, Emma and I met in the courtyard. She was as excited as I was to teach me about self-awareness. We had become great friends, and she wanted the best for me, therefore she put her best efforts in every possible way to help me gain confidence and come out of my shell.

She started by explaining to me the basic definition of self-awareness. She expounded on it, telling me that self-awareness is the ability to recognize and understand our thoughts, emotions, and behaviors and their impact on ourselves and others and the surrounding environment. It involves being conscious of one's strengths, weaknesses, values, beliefs, and motivations. It also includes the ability to reflect on and evaluate our own actions and responses in different situations, allowing for personal growth and development.

I asked her, "Why is it important to be self-aware?"

Her answer amazed me. She mentioned that self-awareness can lead to knowing our values, leading to better decision-making, improved relationships, and a greater understanding of our identity and goals.

Furthermore, she elaborated on how self-awareness can help us understand our emotions and how they affect our thoughts and behavior, leading to better emotional regulation and empathy for others.

She told me that when we are self-aware, we can recognize our strengths and weaknesses, enabling us to make decisions that align with our goals and values. Awareness of our behaviors and reactions can improve our interactions with others, leading to healthier and more meaningful relationships.

It also allows us to recognize areas for improvement in our lives and work toward personal development and growth. She helped me understand the importance of self-awareness by stating it as a means to increase self-confidence. It helps us understand our own abilities and limitations, which can lead to greater self-confidence and assertiveness.

Knowing ourselves helps us identify and develop strategies to manage stress triggers more effectively. Self-aware people can adapt more easily to changes in their environment because they understand their own reactions and can adjust accordingly. Also, being self-aware allows us to live in alignment with our true selves, making choices that reflect our values and beliefs.

By the end of the lesson she explained, "Overall, self-awareness can lead to a more fulfilling and successful life by helping us understand ourselves and navigate the world more effectively."

"I hope you got the essence of the lesson. If there are any questions, ask me right away, without any hesitation."

I took a moment to comprehend what she explained to me. Everything looked confusing for a while, but then it started to make sense. I told her, "I tried to find out what was wrong with me, but I just feel stuck. I want to change and become a better person, a more confident and self-aware one, but I don't know why it seems almost impossible to me."

Emma looked at me carefully, listening to what I was saying.

"I try to think and understand why I behave so awkwardly in front of people and lack self-confidence, but every time I do that, I fail to recognize the causes."

I paused and sighed, "Sometimes I feel like avoiding interaction with everyone! But I guess that's not possible."

With a warm smile on her face, Emma patted the back of my palm lightly as if she were reassuring me.

She said, "Don't worry. It's okay. Don't stress too much; it will take time, but you will improve. I will teach you how to become self-aware and a better version of yourself."

"Really? Is it possible for me to achieve it?"

"Yes, it definitely is!"

"How can I develop self-awareness?" I asked her.

"Well, I must say that it is not entirely easy, and it doesn't come innately, but let me assure you that it is not impossible either," she said. She then continued to expound on it.

"Let's learn about it step-by-step," Emma continued.

She told me that the first thing we should do is to reflect on our experiences. We should think about what we experienced in the past and how it made us feel. Ponder over it, and try to find out the reason behind your feelings and experiences.

Secondly, talking to our trusted friends and family and asking for their feedback can help us determine the areas in our personality that require improvement. Their perspective can help us gain a more objective understanding of ourselves.

In addition, practicing mindfulness can help us determine our thoughts, actions, and emotional behavior without judgment. It can be achieved by practicing meditation or exercises involving deep breathing. It can help you analyze your internal state. Identifying our values and beliefs can help make us more self-aware. Eventually, we can align our actions and behaviors according to our beliefs and values.

In addition, to become self-aware, it is crucial to pay attention to our reactions. How we react to a certain situation or in a certain way tells much about our thought processes and internalized beliefs. Once we start reflecting on how we react, it can help us determine its advantages and disadvantages. Ultimately, gaining self-awareness will enable us to improve our reactions if they need improvement.

Also, self-awareness requires being open to new ideas and challenges, even if they challenge our own. It enables us to look beyond our perceptions and ideas and perceive the world in a new way, thus broadening our mindset.

In addition to becoming self-aware, analyzing ourselves and determining our goals and objectives is essential. It can lead us to personal progress and development, eventually leading us to a more refined and better version of ourselves.

Apart from that, learning from our relationship with people helps us to gain self-awareness, as it reflects how people behave and act in our presence. It improves our behavior around people and helps us establish good relationships with them, improving our social interactions and behavior.

Emma urged me to think outside the box. She gave me a new perspective on my life. She accepted me where I was with love, acceptance, and no judgment. She spoke knowledge and truth into my life and taught me that change is often uncomfortable but necessary for self-development and internal growth. Her love, acceptance, and insight helped break down resistance to change, and now I welcome it. I promised her, "I will do my best to incorporate all of these aspects in myself starting today. I hope that I succeed in this new phase of my life."

"Yes, I am sure that you will do it," Emma assured me.

We both left the courtyard and went to our designated buses, as it was time to go home.

Chapter 5: Empowering Self-Confidence

My interactions with Emma made me think about a lot of things. She didn't only prove to be my friend and my confidant, but she became my biggest supporter. I looked forward to meeting her every day. My days at school were made better, as she was by my side then. I didn't feel alone anymore.

After our self-awareness conversation, I pondered it as much as I could. She made me realize what I lacked and needed to improve in myself. The conversation was eye-opening, and I looked forward to discussing many more aspects of my life with her. We had great talks. Her perspectives and opinions impressed me, and I agreed with almost all of them.

After meeting her, I realized I wanted to improve my former self and had a chance of becoming a better version of myself. We had a lot to discuss, and I eagerly awaited to discuss a new subject with her the next morning. She had already mentioned that we were going to talk about self-confidence.

I didn't want to stress much about it and wanted to take things slow, so I relaxed and went to sleep, leaving everything to be discussed with Emma for the next day.

"Hi, Emma. How are you?"

"I am good," I nodded with a grin. "Did you have a good sleep last night?" she asked.

We met before class the next day and had plenty of time, so we sat and talked for a while. I guess Emma had prepared herself how she would teach me about the importance of self-confidence, the new subject that I wanted to discuss.

"So, it is important for you to know what self-confidence is and how it affects us," Emma said.

I attentively listened to what she had to say.

She continued, "Self-confidence is the belief in our abilities, judgment, and worth. It's the courage to say what you want and think instead of sitting in shame."

"Wait, let me make it easier for you… it is the attitude toward your abilities and capabilities. It is the trust you hold for everything you can do. No one is going to come to save you, so you need to ask yourself, 'What are *you* going to do to make the necessary changes to make things happen?'"

I felt intrigued by what Emma said.

"I get it… but how can we do that?" I asked.

She told me self-confidence involves trusting our capacity to handle challenges, achieve goals, and make decisions. It makes us feel assured in our skills and knowledge, yet also acknowledges the limitations and the areas of improvement. It includes a sense of self-assuredness, resilience, and a positive self-image and influences how we approach and interact with people.

"Wow, that is enlightening," I remarked.

"So, let's dive deep into this…" Emma said excitedly.

We discussed the subject, and I learned some interesting things. I came to understand why self-confidence is important.

It enhances our ability to tackle challenges and improve our overall performance in life. It helps us to improve our communication and interpersonal skills, enabling us to communicate more effectively and assertively.

Additionally, it enables us to make more informed decisions and enhances our confidence in decision-making. Self-confidence helps us recover from setbacks or challenges during decision-making or unfavorable outcomes. It makes us step out of our comfort zone and allows us to try new things, enabling us to take a step forward in life's adventures.

It also lowers stress and anxiety, while fostering a positive mindset, as we look forward confidently to any challenging situation. It allows us to pursue and achieve our objectives and goals. Certainly, being self-confident helps us achieve what we want. Therefore, it increases our chances of having a fulfilling life.

"I hope I made it easy for you to understand. Trust me, it sounds intimidating at first, but it will get easier with time," Emma reassured.

"I can't wait to learn how to gain self-confidence." I showed my enthusiasm, and Emma continued to enlighten me about it.

First, she told me that achieving small, attainable goals builds a sense of accomplishment and confidence. We can also replace negative self-talk with positive affirmations and reframe critical thoughts. It will make us look beyond the possibilities of failures and focus on the positive outcome.

Moreover, taking care of our physical and mental health through exercise, healthy eating, and rest can restore self-confidence. When we feel good on the outside, it also makes us feel better on the inside.

Visualizing ourselves succeeding also reassures our self-confidence. When we picture ourselves succeeding in various situations, we do ourselves a favor as it builds more confidence. Additionally, being well-prepared can boost our confidence in specific tasks or situations.

It is natural and normal to endure hardships or challenges when we are on the path to success. View challenges as opportunities to learn and grow rather than as threats. This not only builds self-confidence but also ensures self-reliance if we fail. Whenever we succeed, we must recognize and reward ourselves for successes, big or small, because celebrating our success boosts our self-confidence.

To build our self-confidence, we should spend time with supportive and encouraging individuals. These people not only support us when we fail but also celebrate our achievements with us. They make us feel that we are worthy despite our failures or achievements. Most of the time people only stay by our side when we succeed, but whenever we fail, we are often left alone, making us question our worth.

Furthermore, stepping out of our comfort zone and facing fears can help us build resilience and confidence. We can also consider seeking advice from a mentor, coach, or therapist for additional guidance and support.

The last thing that Emma told me made me realize that I did the right thing by contacting her for mentorship. I was already on my path to building self-confidence, and it kindled a ray of hope inside me.

"From now on, you need to take a stand for yourself. If anyone bothers you or bullies you, or you feel you are being mistreated, stand up for yourself and let others know that you will not be disrespected."

I listened to Emma carefully. I believe that she had a valid point. It all started to make sense! I had never stood up for myself because I lacked self-confidence! She explained that confidence is the by-product of taking action, so it's important to take action even if you feel insecure.

The more you take action and say what's on your mind, the easier it gets every time you do it. And the more you do it, the more people will understand you and begin to know you. Emma explained how I should raise my voice against anything unfair, be it to me personally or to anyone else. I learned that using our voice effectively involves expressing ourselves clearly and confidently in different situations.

Speaking clearly and directly is important to be understood and to get your point across.

It is important to set our tone and pitch. Sometimes it helps convey emotions and emphasize what we wish to convey.

When we raise our voices for anything, we must compose ourselves confidently. Our body language exhibits how strong or confident we appear, which is important when leaving an impression.

It is essential to voice our opinions, but it is also crucial to watch our tone and choose words that convey respect and positivity, especially when providing feedback or addressing disagreements. Also, managing our emotions when speaking, especially in challenging situations, is significant in maintaining control of our voice.

Raising our voice is an important aspect of public speaking. It is not only used against any bias or prejudice, but it is also important for regular public speaking. So, practicing how to speak and what to say in public beforehand might help us when we have to face someone. Practice by writing down what you want to say on paper, and then look in the mirror. Practice by speaking clearly and firmly, conveying the message you want, and paying attention to your body and facial language. Using our voice effectively, we can communicate persuasively, build strong relationships, and achieve our goals. We can also stand against any bias or injustice towards us or anyone else.

"You can start today by participating confidently in class. Also, confront Coach Shane and ask him to let you shoot the ball instead of Bethany," Emma said after she explained everything about raising my inner voice.

"I am giving you a task for today. You need to raise your voice during your practice session today. Go and ask for what you want. You are an excellent basketball player!" Emma pushed me.

"I am not sure if I can do this," I said nervously.

"Don't listen to your negative self-talk. You have to! This is your task. Only then you will be able to regain your self-confidence."

"Okay, I am gonna give it a try."

"Let me also tell you about your inner voice. It is an important part of our personalities and everybody has one," she said.

Turning the volume up on our inner voice helps us reflect on our thoughts, feelings, and actions, leading to greater self-awareness and understanding. We can manage our emotions more effectively and maintain emotional balance by listening to our inner voice. In addition, our inner voice can guide us in making decisions that align with our values and goals. It can help us tap into our intuition and gain deeper insights. Engaging with our inner voice allows us to think through challenges and find solutions, boosting our confidence and self-esteem. It can also help us recognize when to set boundaries in relationships and situations.

When we turn up the volume of our inner voice, take steps forward, and stay consistent, we develop good habits that help us reach our goals over time. Using our inner voice can lead to a more mindful and intentional approach to life, helping us navigate challenges and achieve our goals.

"You can find your inner voice by analyzing yourself, Claire. Think about what your mind is saying to you in a tough situation. Scrutinize your reactions to things and ask yourself if your reactions are healthy. Listen to your mind and your heart and act accordingly. You should also set boundaries when you feel uncomfortable. It will keep you safe from any unnecessary pain or hurt."

"Listen to what your inner voice says and act upon it. You will thank me later," she said with a subtle wink.

The bell rang, and it was time for our class. Before I could say anything else, Emma got up and said, "Let's go, Claire."

While walking towards the class, I contemplated how I was going to participate in class that day. I prepared myself to be more self-confident and answer questions, even if I didn't know the right answer. I knew then that I needed to take action, even though I felt insecure. I constantly reminded myself about everything that Emma taught me.

To my surprise, I answered many questions Ms. Reid asked that day. I got some answers incorrect but didn't let that affect me, and I looked forward to others.

Soon the class ended, and Emma met me outside.

"Whoa, that was impressive. You are such a quick learner," she remarked.

I felt exhilarated.

"Now, it's time for the next task of the day."

"Yeah… I know." I said sarcastically.

"I know you can do this too."

Emma's words reassured me that I could stand up for myself against Coach Shane and Bethany. We walked toward the basketball court. Emma sat on one of the benches while I changed in the locker room.

While I changed, I continuously reminded myself of the goal I had in mind, that I had to stand up for my rights. It was not fair that Coach Shane always had Bethany shoot the three-point shot and not me.

After changing, I went straight to Coach Shane.

"Hello, Coach. I want to play in my spot today and shoot the three-point shot instead of Bethany. I understand that she is your niece, but you cannot be unfair to me," I said respectfully, yet sternly.

Coach Shane was stunned. He was not expecting what he was hearing. He stood there speechless for a couple of seconds. I continued to say,

"If you will not let me play, I might go to the principal…"

I hadn't even finished my sentence when he said,

"It's okay. You will play and shoot the three-pointer."

I was shocked.

"Wow, that was easy," I thought to myself.

The rest of the practice session went well. Emma watched everything and waited for me after the practice.

"You did it, girl! I am so proud of you," she exclaimed.

I felt a strange sense of relief and contentment, which I hadn't felt in a while. I didn't know that standing up for myself would give me so much strength. It had been a while since I had felt so powerful and brave.

"Thank you so much, Emma. I really appreciate you helping me find my voice and speak up!"

"You are welcome, my friend. It is going to be much better. Just be patient."

It was time to go home then. I went and settled in on my bus. A wave of joy and fulfillment had taken over me. I felt it all the way home.

Chapter 6: The Power of Kindness and Empathy

It was the start of a new day for me, filled with anticipation, as I looked forward to discussing a new topic with Emma.

The morning began with the gentle sound of my alarm clock waking me up. Light was peeking through the curtains, signaling the beginning of a new day. I got up from my bed and stretched before walking into the bathroom. I washed my face, brushed my teeth, and combed my hair. I was feeling relaxed and less anxious. After getting ready for the day, I went down the stairs to the kitchen for a quick breakfast of cereal and toast.

Once I had eaten, I gathered my things and headed out the door to catch my bus. The morning air felt crisp and fresh as I set off for school, ready to take on the day.

The positive change I felt inside myself was surreal and hard to believe. My boost of confidence and self-assurance was inexplicably astounding. Asking Emma for mentorship was the best thing I had done in a long time.

I reached school on time and waited for Emma before class. A couple of minutes later, I saw her walking toward me through the hallway.

"Hey, Claire. How are you, buddy?" She asked loudly from a distance.

"I am good. How are you?" I responded with a beam as she approached me.

"Do you want to know what I have prepared for you today? It is going to be exciting."

"Yes, please. Tell me." I was curious.

I knew she must have planned something useful and informative.

"Today, I am going to tell you about empathy and kindness," she said eagerly. "Are you up for it?"

"I sure am. Let's do it before class. We still have some time left until Ms. Reid comes."

"Come on, let's go!"

We went to the same spot where we sat yesterday and started to talk.

"I am sure you must know what empathy and kindness are…"

"Yes, Emma. I know that *empathy* is to feel, understand, and consider what the other person is feeling. It means being sensitive to others and being aware of their feelings and emotions," I paused, "And I guess *kindness* is somewhat similar. It means to be friendly, generous, and considerate with a person. It refers to the quality and actions of being gentle, caring, and helpful when it comes to somebody else."

Emma smiled and looked at me as I spoke. Her eyes shone as if she was proud of something.

"I am impressed, Claire. That was admirable. You know so much about it already. I think I don't have to tell you a lot about it," she laughed.

The feeling of somebody being impressed and proud of me felt new to me. The shell I lived in before didn't give me a chance to make someone proud. I guess it was because of the boost of self-confidence and self-assurance I had gained after Emma's previous lessons.

"I think it's working…" I said,

"What is working?" Emma asked, confused.

"Your mentorship," I chuckled.

"Oh, yes. I am glad!" Emma laughed. "Let's get back to where we left off. You already know what these two qualities are. You should use them as your superpowers."

What? *Superpowers?* How is that possible? I thought. Just then, Emma started to explain how.

Emma told me that empathy is a virtue that teaches us to be kind and compassionate. Empathy and kindness both go hand-in-hand. When we are empathetic towards others, we are in the process of being kind, and if we are kind towards others, that means we are naturally empathetic.

Being empathetic doesn't mean feeling sorry for others, but it shows compassion and understanding. Being empathetic is sensing other people's emotions and feelings and trying to understand what another is feeling and experiencing. It is the ability to imagine and experience the inner world of another person, identifying what the other person is feeling at a given time, imagining what someone is thinking, recognizing and validating their emotions, listening to what they have to say, imagining how the other person might be feeling, and seeing things from their point of view.

On the other hand, kindness is a quality that can work wonders. Kindness enables us to be selfless, compassionate, considerate, and generous. It is a quality that spreads positivity and generosity. It is a chain that prevails in society. Being kind to someone is to be considerate of their feelings and needs. It is a way to show sincerity and thoughtfulness. Small gestures or words can show kindness. Kindness can be expressed by showing the other person that you care for them. It is showing goodness, goodwill, courtesy, concern, and grace. It is being patient, loving, helpful, and hospitable. It is being unselfish or self-centered and being tolerant and understanding.

Kindness and empathy can make a lot of difference in society. They are like superpowers. When we make them a part of our lives, we make a difference for others and ourselves. They provide a sense of fulfillment and purpose. They make us feel satisfied, pleased, and content with how we behave and react to someone else. Choosing to be kind helps us grow as individuals.

When we choose to be kind and empathetic, we are living in the other person's mind and heart. Thus, it acts like a superpower because not everybody can do so. Special people practice kindness and empathy. The people who have engraved these two qualities in themselves are superheroes who can relate to and understand someone else's mind and heart.

When she stopped, I started absorbing everything she said, thinking about how to include these practices in my life.

"Have you ever thought about how you can use these qualities in your daily life?" Emma asked.

"Umm… not really. I am not sure. I don't usually interact with people a lot, so I don't think about them often. I wouldn't say I am rude, mean, or unkind. I try to be empathetic and kind, but I don't have the courage or confidence to interact with people in such a way."

As far as I knew, I had the instinct of empathy and kindness, but my lack of self-confidence and courage never made me attempt it. I would think of helping people in need but would stay silent because I wasn't confident enough to stand up to people.

Even when I saw my friend being bullied, I stood afar in silence because I feared the consequences and the reaction of the bullies. I could have helped her in that situation, but my lack of confidence prevented me from doing so.

After what Emma taught me, I decided to incorporate these qualities into my daily life no matter what. I had started to gain my self-confidence back, so I was hopeful I would embed kindness and empathy into my personality as well.

Moving on to the topic, Emma explained to me how to use them in my daily life.

Kindness and empathy are powerful tools that can positively impact our daily lives and the lives of those around us. We can be kind and empathetic by listening actively. It is very kind to pay full attention when someone is speaking to us. Show interest, respond thoughtfully, and help make the other person feel heard and valued.

Recognizing and acknowledging the strengths, talents, and efforts of those around us is a very warm gesture. A simple compliment can brighten someone's day, so we should incorporate giving compliments to others into our lives.

Besides that, give others time and space to express themselves. Avoid rushing people, and show understanding if they are struggling. Being considerate, patient, and tolerant can make a notable impact.

Also, we should express gratitude and appreciation for other people and things we encounter each day. A thank-you note or a verbal expression of thanks can mean a lot to others. Being hospitable and making an effort for somebody also counts as kindness and empathy. Letting people know that we are there for them in times of need is quite reassuring. Validating their feelings and offering comfort without judgment might seem like a tiny act of kindness, but it goes a long way!

The most commonly-practiced gesture of empathy and kindness is helping others. It can be something big that holds a lot of meaning, requires effort, or even anything tiny or mundane. Look for opportunities to lend a hand, whether it's holding a door open, offering to carry something, or helping someone in need.

It is important to choose language that is considerate and respectful. We should avoid negative comments and be cautious about how our words may affect others because sometimes words can be very hurtful.

Moreover, practicing random acts of kindness and empathy can make someone's day. Do something kind without expecting anything in return. It can be as simple as paying for someone's coffee or leaving a kind note for a colleague.

Furthermore, we should be mindful that respecting people's boundaries is essential. It is important to understand and respect the limits and preferences of others, whether it involves personal space or emotional boundaries.

Demonstrating kindness and empathy in our interactions with others can inspire others to do the same. By consciously practicing kindness and empathy in our daily lives, we can build stronger relationships, contribute to a positive community, and enhance our own well-being.

"I am giving you a task today. You have to use these two qualities daily in some way throughout the week. I will be with you, so you don't have to worry about anything," Emma said.

When I first heard about the exercise, I was intimidated. I was a bit relieved when Emma said she would help me throughout though. I was excited and scared but ready to take on my task.

Soon, it was time for class, and we saw Ms. Reid approaching. Emma and I went inside the classroom and settled down.

The rest of the day went pretty well. I also thought about how I could help others and be empathetic toward them.

We left the classroom and walked through the hallway. Emma asked me to be observant of my surroundings. This way, I could see if anyone required my help. She gave me an example through my basketball sessions. I could help my teammates by assisting them in warming up or stretching, or I could help them by teaching them how to shoot a ball correctly. She told me to look around whenever I was walking on the road. I can help somebody elderly or weak. I could hold doors for people who were walking in and out of a store. I could help somebody carry their bags to the car if they cannot do it alone. She told me so many things I could do to show kindness to others.

She explained to me that kindness is offering grace. We are humans, and therefore, we make mistakes. We can be kind in our response to ourselves and others when those mistakes occur. This means thinking before speaking, thinking before seeking revenge, and thinking about long-term relationships instead of short-term pride. If we could all remember that none of us are perfect, we would all be kinder to each other. Offer grace and be kind.

I learned that it's not only our opinion that matters. We should respect other people's opinions and respectfully disagree with them if we don't agree. We should be appreciative and grateful. We should be tolerant and patient.

Emma taught me a lot and asked me to incorporate those details into my daily life. I promised to do so no matter where I would be throughout the day.

Throughout the week, I clung to Emma's words and looked around myself to help people. The next day, on my way back home from the supermarket, I saw an old lady struggling to carry her bags and open the door simultaneously. I was quite far from the door, but I ran to open the door for her. She looked at me and smiled.

"So kind of you. Thank you so much!"

When I heard those words, I felt so happy. It felt like it was the best thing I had done in a while. Even when I went back and went to bed, I kept thinking about the little sentence she said to me.

"Ah! This feels good," I murmured to myself.

I had never felt such contentment in my life. I started to help out around the house as well. I would help my Mom and

Dad cook, do the dishes, clean the house, do laundry, or mow the lawn. I really liked helping them with everything.

I helped Abby, my younger sister, with her homework, and Eve, my older sister, with her science projects. I spoke to them more kindly and became more tolerant and patient whenever we quarreled.

I helped my friends at school. I realized the kindest, bravest thing we can do is stand up to someone who is being unkind. Doing so causes conflict. A nice person would see the potential for conflict and stay quiet. A nice person never wants to rock the boat. A kind and courageous person knows conflict is possible and acts anyway. They know they might create waves, but they are okay with that. I also gave a tough time to the bullies throughout the week and warned them not to mess with my friends.

When I decided to be kind and empathetic, it was like I was living a new life. It seemed like I had a purpose and felt like I wasn't just existing. I felt alive and happy. I was satisfied with helping people and being more empathetic. It was powerful. I guess Emma was right about using them as my *superpowers*.

I learned that being kind and empathetic habitually is important for several reasons. It strengthens our relationships because kindness and empathy help build strong and meaningful relationships with others. When we show care and understanding toward others, it fosters trust and deepens the connections. Being kind and empathetic can boost our own emotional well-being. It can lead to greater happiness and satisfaction, as helping others often brings a sense of fulfillment.

Additionally, habitual kindness and empathy create a positive atmosphere in personal and professional settings. People are more likely to respond positively and reciprocate when we treat them with kindness and understanding. It also reduces stress and conflicts. Dealing with different situations with empathy can help de-escalate potential conflicts and misunderstandings. It can also reduce our own stress by promoting more harmonious interactions with the people around us.

Kindness and empathy contribute to a supportive and inclusive community. By being considerate of the feelings and perspectives of others, we tend to create an environment where people feel valued and respected. We also set a good example for other people, as demonstrating kindness and empathy can inspire others to do the same. This can create a ripple effect, leading to more compassionate and respectful behavior in our social circles.

When we practice empathy, we become a better listener and communicator. This can lead to more open and honest conversations and improve our ability to understand and address the needs of others. Empathy helps us to see things from a different perspective. It enables us to be more considerate of others instead of being selfish, and it allows us to acknowledge other people's perspectives, even if we don't have to agree with them. It can lead to a greater appreciation for diversity and different perspectives and can contribute to a more inclusive and equitable society.

I concluded that being kind and empathetic benefits others and contributes to our happiness and overall well-being. It creates a positive impact on our relationships and the broader community. I felt grateful to Emma for teaching me so much about this superpower which I didn't know I possessed.

Chapter 7: The Power of Courage and Vulnerability

I had thought of what I was going to talk about to Emma next — those hard and complex feelings I had always found difficult to talk about before. I had a hope of change, desiring to break the pattern and talk about them.

This time I told her what I wanted to talk about, and she liked the enthusiasm and was impressed by how I was initiating to participate.

We both met at the school, thrilled and pumped up for the next session.

"So… fasten your seatbelt, Claire. We are going to talk about uncomfortable feelings and complex topics," Emma said jokingly.

"Let's do this!" I agreed enthusiastically.

"You must know what hard feelings and complex topics are, but you find it difficult to share them and talk about them, right?"

And… we started talking. Emma started teaching me about hard and uncomfortable feelings, explaining how they affect us if we don't talk about them. Talking about these feelings and complex topics can be challenging for several reasons.

One of the reasons is emotional discomfort. Often, addressing uncomfortable feelings brings up painful emotions like sadness, anger, or fear, so many people prefer to avoid these emotions, leading to avoidance of the topic altogether. The feelings build up inside us and can cause frustration and resentment.

Sometimes we are also afraid of judgment. We worry about how others will perceive us if we reveal our true feelings. There is a fear of being judged, misunderstood, or even rejected for expressing thoughts or emotions that are perceived as negative or unpopular.

Some of us also struggle with not knowing how to communicate effectively because we haven't been taught or we don't have the communication skills required to express ourselves or generally express our concerns about something in particular. Therefore, expressing complex emotions and thoughts requires effective communication skills, including articulating feelings, listening actively, and responding empathetically. Not everyone possesses these skills, which can make it difficult to engage in meaningful conversations about difficult topics.

Opening up about uncomfortable feelings requires vulnerability, which can be scary. The fear of being vulnerable is a struggle because it involves exposing ourselves to the possibility of hurt, judgment, or rejection. Our cultural and societal norms often dictate what is considered appropriate or acceptable to discuss openly. Certain topics may be deemed taboo or off limits, making it challenging to bring them up in a conversation.

She also told me that negative past experiences with discussing hard feelings or complex topics, such as being invalidated or dismissed, can create barriers to future communication on similar subjects.

Overall, I learned through this discussion with Emma that addressing hard feelings and complex topics requires courage, empathy, and effective communication skills, all of which can be difficult to cultivate. However, engaging in these conversations can lead to deeper understanding, emotional growth, and stronger connections with others.

I was intrigued by our discussion, so I asked Emma, "How can I develop the courage in myself to talk about these things in my life? I often get extremely intimidated by these kinds of situations."

"I know it is not easy to be outspoken or confident enough to raise your voice, but Claire, for your personal growth, it is something you have to do," she said, "I will tell you how you can develop these aspects of your personality. And trust me, you can do it!"

Uncomfortable conversations help you clarify your thoughts and feelings so that another person can see you in greater depth and understand you better. When we talk about complex feelings and emotions, it provides us relief and releases the emotions that have been bottled up inside us for a long time.

Not talking about these emotions can lead to increased stress and anxiety, which is harmful to our mental and physical health. When we process these emotions sensibly and express them maturely, we get rid of them, along with all the dangerous stress and anxiety. Expressing these emotions can liberate us from frustration, anxiety, and resentment, making us feel free and relaxed. It can be profoundly healing over time to share and discuss uncomfortable feelings with someone we trust, thereby reducing stress and strengthening our immune system.

When we open up about complex situations and hard feelings in a relationship, we instill a sense of trust, empathy, and connection in the bond we share with our partner. This bond forms a deeper connection as we connect on an emotional level. This fosters love, trust, and compassion, eventually strengthening the bond.

It also polishes our problem-solving skills. When we share our concerns and problems with a trusted partner or a confidant, we somehow open ourselves to receive diverse perspectives and insights on a particular topic. These insights allow us to look into the situation in a different way.

Emma expounded how sharing our feelings and discussing topics we often find difficult to talk about facilitates our personal growth. It fosters our development and allows us to grow and evolve. We are able to confront our fears, biases, and misconceptions, and it also enables us to be self-aware and promotes resilience.

When we talk about certain topics that are considered taboo in our society, like societal issues, injustice, prejudice, and inequality, we strive for social change. We participate to raise awareness and bring about a change in the society. All the new information I received from Emma opened a new and diverse perspective on this subject. I learned that it promotes emotional well-being, promotes self-awareness, enhances personal growth and development, and leads to social change.

"Wow, that was informative, Emma. I knew a little about it, but you opened my eyes. There is so much more to know about these feelings," I said, "I never thought of it in this way."

"I am glad, Claire, but now you must allow yourself to speak about anything that you found difficult previously," Emma responded, "I know it is going to be a little difficult in the beginning, but I assure you, it will get better,"

Emma and I talked about what factors we should consider when we express ourselves. When we discuss hard feelings and complex topics, several considerations can help us ensure a constructive and respectful conversation and avoid any hurtful and uncomfortable encounters.

The first thing we should do is to choose empathy. Approaching the conversation with empathy and understanding and acknowledging that everyone experiences emotions differently will surely help you to have a positive outcome. It ensures peace and harmony, avoids any distressing situations, and promotes patience.

In such situations, when the other person is speaking or expressing themselves, it is essential to instill and practice active listening by giving our full attention to the other person while listening, without interrupting or judging.

Reflecting on what we have heard to ensure mutual understanding, identifying where we can express our opinions and concerns, and looking forward to a healthy conversation and outcome are examples of mature behavior.

Be it any situation, it is essential to treat others' viewpoints with respect, even if we disagree. What we can do best is to avoid dismissive language or invalidating someone else's experiences. Through this, we can contribute to creating a safe space where everyone feels comfortable expressing themselves without fear of judgment or retaliation. We can also establish ground rules, if necessary, to maintain respectful communication. Also, keeping an open mind and being willing to consider perspectives that differ from our own allows us to look at different opinions and perspectives. We should also allow ourselves to be curious and ask questions to deepen our understanding.

We must respect personal boundaries and only share what we feel comfortable disclosing. Similarly, respect the boundaries of others, if they choose not to share certain information, and never try to intrude. We must also keep in mind that we should use language that is inclusive and non-judgmental, avoid stereotypes or assumptions, and be mindful of how our words may impact others.

We must be aware of emotional regulation and try our best to control and maintain it when we are discussing anything crucial or complex. We should recognize when our emotions are running high and take a step back to de-escalate, if necessary, because escalating situations or conversations might result in an unpleasant end of the conversation.

Aim for understanding and resolution rather than winning arguments. Seek common ground and focus on finding solutions or compromises where possible.

By considering these factors, we can foster a constructive conversation that promotes empathy, understanding, and mutual respect when discussing hard feelings and complex topics.

Our conversation ended leaving me feeling enlightened.

"I might be able to express myself more now," I mentioned.

"I am certain," Emma responded, looking at me with a smile on her face as if she was proud of me.

"You know what, Emma? I cannot wait to apply everything that you told me. I feel so liberated."

"That's amazing, Claire. I know you are capable of it!"

These words sounded like a melody to my ears. I had never heard these reassuring words often before, and neither had I explored this side of mine.

It was new, but it was good.

"Okay, come on, get up! Let's go and have lunch. I am famished." Emma interrupted my intrusive thoughts.

Snapping back to reality, I got up and joined Emma, who was already a few steps ahead of me.

Chapter 8: The Power of Finding Your Voice and Speaking Up

As time went by, Emma and I became great friends. Not only was she my mentor now, but she became someone I could confide in. I had a true friend after a long time, maybe for the first time in my life.

Emma taught me so much that I didn't know, but felt I should have known about it earlier. If I had been aware of it before, my life would have been so much different and better.

However, I didn't waste my time regretting the past, and I looked at the future with the hope of personal development and progress.

Every day came with a ray of hope and a desire to learn something new and achieve something that I hadn't previously, be it mundane or tiny or anything that holds a lot of importance. If it didn't hold the utmost importance in the eyes of some people, for me, it made a great difference, and that is what mattered the most.

I looked forward to meeting Emma the next day.

It was a clear Wednesday morning. I reached school earlier than Emma and waited for her to meet me in the corridor. I saw her coming towards me, with a wide and bright smile on her face.

"Hey, Emma, how are you?"

"Claire, I am good. I hope you are well too. Come on, let's go and talk about today's topic."

Emma and I walked towards a silent corner and got seated.

"We are going to discuss your voice today."

"My voice?" I asked curiously.

"I meant your literal voice that allows you to speak up and advocate for yourself. That voice."

"Oh...I see."

I was pumped to learn about my voice. I learned that we all have a voice, which means we have a right to express our opinions, thoughts, and feelings. Our inner voice allows us to recognize our thoughts and perspectives and regard the perspectives of other people too. It is a concept associated with equality, freedom of speech, and inclusion. It highlights what matters to us and helps us express ourselves and our opinions.

"Now, that is some interesting stuff," I said.

Emma had told me about this previously, and now she wanted me to find my own voice.

I agreed to it and promised her to try my best to express my thoughts and opinions.

I had been a shy girl all my life, but now it was time to change this trait of mine. I knew it would be a little difficult in the beginning, but I had to find the courage to overcome the inability to express myself. Speaking up and using your voice is the root of all social changes. For many of us, it is easier to advocate for others than it is to speak up for ourselves. We erode our sense of self-worth when we don't speak up for ourselves.

Everyone has a voice of their own that allows them to express themselves and let their opinions be known. Our voices can make a lot of difference for us and for other people. By speaking the facts and the truth, we can help ourselves to be recognized, to achieve, to accomplish, and not be wronged in any way. Similarly, this goes for others too. We might see people around us being wronged or not being recognized for what they do. People often suffer to achieve what they deserve and get wronged in many different ways.

By using our voices, we can help people get out of such situations. By raising our voices the right way, we can make a difference in society by helping ourselves and others achieve what we deserve.

I acknowledged that I should help people around me, regardless of their background, age, ethnicity, and culture. I should always be aware of my inner voice and be willing and able to express it whenever it is needed.

I remember watching my friend being bullied by some of my classmates but never saying anything and leaving the place silently. However, I wanted to take a stand and help her in this distressing situation, but I never had the courage to confront anyone, so I walked away. Similarly, I remembered another incident where raising my voice for what was right and good could have made a difference, but I failed as usual.

My classmate, Lucy, borrowed *The Treasure Island* from the library. In our next unit in the library, we were told about the same book being lost. The librarian interrogated Lucy in front of everyone, accusing her that she hadn't returned the book, however I remembered that she had returned the book. I had seen her giving it back to the librarian as I was behind her in the queue. We were all intimidated by the situation, as the librarian rudely questioned Lucy in front of the class, accusing her of misplacing the book and telling her she would be fined if it was not found by the next day. I looked at Lucy. She was terrified and looked as if she was about to cry. I heard her explaining herself, saying that she had returned the book on the due date, but the librarian didn't believe her. I could have spoken up at that moment, testifying that she had returned the book, but I couldn't speak up because of my lack of self-confidence and self-assurance.

The bell rang, and everyone left the library. Lucy stood there in silence, pondering the situation. An expression of panic was evident on her face. I approached her and asked, "Are you okay, Lucy?"

"I don't know what to do now. I returned it on the due date. I feel ashamed, being accused of something I didn't do," she said, her voice low and broken.

"I know you returned it," I said hesitantly.

She looked at me with horror, as if she was disappointed and heartbroken.

"You should have said something then," she said sternly.

"I… I… don't know what I should have said." I stumbled upon my words. "I am sorry, Lucy."

I left the library, leaving Lucy alone to find the book.

The next day, one of our mutual friends told me that the book was found in the librarian's drawer. I was relieved to hear it, yet I was ashamed too. If I had spoken up, Lucy would have felt a sense of relief and support. Guilt had taken over me. I felt embarrassed and like a coward. However, I numbed my feelings and went on with the rest of the day, immersed in insecurities and guilt. What Lucy had felt yesterday, I kept on thinking, what if I had spoken up for her? If I had, she wouldn't have had to go through all that mess!

This incident worked as an example for me to know the importance of speaking up and raising my voice to express the truth. I mentioned it to Emma and looked forward to what she had to say.

"It is high time that you should know to find your voice and use it for good. You must speak the truth, Claire. Often, it is petrifying, but you should remember that truth always prevails."

I nodded in agreement. Emma continued to tell me how I could find my voice.

Finding your voice and speaking the truth involves a journey of self-discovery and developing the courage to express yourself authentically.

To make a point and express yourself, it is essential to spend time reflecting on your values, beliefs, and experiences. Identify what matters most to you and what you stand for. It is crucial to educate yourself on the topics and issues that are important to you. What you can do is read, research, and engage with diverse perspectives to deepen your understanding.

In addition, practice self-awareness and be mindful of your thoughts and emotions. This will develop self-confidence and self-assurance. You will be convinced that you are worthy and that your opinion matters.

Also, it is important to determine the best way for you to communicate, whether through writing, speaking, art, or another form of expression. You can also experiment with different formats to find what resonates with you.

Once you get a hold of it, ask for feedback from trusted sources like friends, mentors, or peers. They might also be able to give you different and valuable insights which will probably help you find a more refined version of your voice.

Apart from that, be true to yourself and avoid conforming to the expectations of society. Your focus should be on authenticity, building credibility and trust with your audience. Trying to engage in meaningful conversations with different people around you will enable you to expand your ideas and maintain your stance when speaking publicly. You might make mistakes in the beginning, but with time, you will learn to use your voice impactfully and effectively.

You must work on these aspects and be patient during the ongoing process. Everything requires a certain amount of time, and you will succeed in maintaining your voice and using it to make an impact in society. By following these steps, you can develop the ability to speak your truth with clarity and conviction, making a positive impact on those around you.

Speaking the truth might seem daunting in the beginning. You might be terrified of stating the facts or truth, but it gets easier with time. Once the fact is established that truth holds the utmost power, it becomes easy for us to say it out loud, even if it gets difficult.

Sometimes, the situation might get complex, and you can get yourself in trouble, but sticking to the truth always wins. Be fearless and state the truth even if your voice shakes.

Stay committed to your words, and say them with confidence. Know that you are on the right side, and nothing can beat the truth. Lies or deceit is short-lived, but the truth is the ultimate triumph. The satisfaction and fulfillment you achieve after speaking the truth or helping someone in a complex situation is exceptionally comforting and fulfilling. Truth is powerful, and it makes you resilient and courageous.

The facts about truth blew my mind. It came as a shocking revelation which I had never paid attention to. It instilled a sense of awakening in me, and I decided not to stay silent anymore. I was determined to tell the truth no matter what circumstances I faced. I knew that it was going to be a little difficult in the beginning, but I knew that with determination and consistency, it would become easier. This determination made me focus on helping myself and others and standing up for myself and others when needed.

"Emma, that was enlightening. I am going to work on it, and you will surely notice my progress," I said with determination.

"You can do it, I am certain, Claire. Remember to be focused and resilient, and don't back off until your work is done," Emma said confidently.

Appreciation and reassurance from Emma always made me feel at the top of the world. I had never felt this way with any of my friends or family. It felt like a fresh beginning to my new-found personality. Overjoyed and exhilarated, I looked forward to progress and striving to become my best self.

Chapter 9: The Dance of Liberation - Gratitude and Friendship

It was the beginning of May, and everyone was excited about the upcoming event at our school, including Emma and myself. The *spring formal dance* was just around the corner. The event was already the talk of the school, and everyone was waiting impatiently for the 5th of May. Preparations for the dance were in full swing, and everyone was busy preparing for it.

It was the first time I was thrilled about the dance since I started attending the school. Along with our mentoring sessions, we went to buy our dresses. From our outfits to our hairstyles, we had decided everything. Emma and I chose similar outfits and matching updo hairstyles.

In the blink of an eye, it was the night before the *spring formal dance*. I had invited Emma over to my house so we could get ready together for the event. Emma's mother dropped her off at my house on the evening of the dance. She brought her beautiful rose gown, and I had a similar one in a soft blue color. My room had turned into a salon as we both began to get ready for the event. Emma and I had a lot of fun while getting ready, from doing each other's makeup to styling our hair into sleek buns.

By 6:00 p.m. in the evening, we were ready to attend the spring formal dance. My mother dropped us off at the school.

The journey to school seemed to pass quickly, as we were giddy with excitement.

Emma and I stepped out of the car as we reached school, picking up our gowns so they didn't touch the ground. Our hearts raced, and our eyes sparkled with excitement. We stepped into the community hall. The vibe of the hall was exhilarating. The ceiling lit up, lights glimmering, and loud music played in the background with everyone on the dance floor. We took a second to appreciate the sights and sounds before we moved forward.

Emma and I were on the dance floor, enjoying ourselves as we danced and giggled at each other's dance moves. More of our friends, including Lucy, joined us in the dance. It was such a fun moment with everyone around me. My newly-instilled confidence allowed me to enjoy myself and express myself among people.

After the dance, everyone had snacks arranged by the dance committee. What a feast it was. Yogurt, granola, yummy donuts, grilled chicken kebabs, and a huge fruit platter. I ate everything that night. The confidence and self-assurance could even be seen in my appetite.

After we finished eating, Emma approached me and asked, "How are you doing, Claire? How have you been?"

"I feel liberated, Emma. It feels so refreshing and new to be living like this. It felt like I was missing out on living a healthy life. I never knew that self-confidence and self-assurance are that important in our lives."

Emma listened to me carefully, with a soft smile on her face. I could already tell she was proud of me.

"You know what, Claire… I am so proud of you. I knew from the beginning that you could do it. The potential you had was evident from the start. I love how you have dealt with everything. You should be proud of your courage, determination, and resilience. You just needed a push, and that is what I did."

"Thank you, Emma. You are the only true friend I have ever had in my life."

"You are always welcome, Claire. And you know what? I found a friend in you too."

Emma and I felt safe and confident around each other. She was the friend I had been looking for forever.

As the night ended with our final dance of the year, flashbacks of everything I had learned over the year replayed in my mind. With a wide grin on my face, feeling alive and liberated, I went over each and every thing that Emma taught me.

I reminisced about how she taught me about self-worth and its significance. I realized my self-worth, which ultimately helped me gain self-confidence and provided me with self-assurance, drastically boosting my self-worth.

My sessions with Emma taught me about kindness, empathy, and compassion. I became empathetic and compassionate toward people. I focused more on helping people and treating them with care and love, and I found a drastic shift in my relationship dynamics. Relations with my family and friends also improved when I embarked on the journey of kindness and empathy.

I also learned to communicate my complicated feelings and share the emotions and thoughts that were difficult for me to express to others. Earlier, I never used to express how I felt or what bothered me, but I started learning to speak about it and felt free from all the negative emotions accumulated inside of me. I learned to speak up and raise my inner voice.

It infused me with immense knowledge and insight about the things I should have known from the start. It brought me an exceptional enlightenment that transformed my personality drastically. I learned to use my voice for the right reasons, which not only helped me, but also the people around me. I began to stand up for my friends and myself. I felt powerful once I started voicing my thoughts.

Emma and I were exhausted by the end of the night, but we had so much fun. It was one of the best nights of my life. Deep down in my heart, I didn't want it to end. We enjoyed ourselves as much as possible and danced our hearts out without thinking about our surroundings. It felt like nobody was watching me and I was free. But it was time to go home now.

My mother had to pick us up, so Emma and I rushed to the main entrance.

"Wait… before we go out and the school year ends, I want to tell you one important thing."

"What is that, Emma?"

"Always remember to be grateful. It will take you a long way."

Just before Mom came to pick us up, Emma told me about this one thing before we left the spring dance.

Being grateful means feeling thankful for the good things in our lives. It is more than just saying "thank you" out of habit. It is about truly appreciating what we have and the people around us. When we express gratitude, we enable ourselves to focus on what we have instead of what we don't. This simple shift in thinking can make a big difference in how happy and satisfied we feel.

When we practice gratitude, we start to notice the little things that make life enjoyable. It might be a sunny day, a good meal, or a kind word from a friend. We can find happiness in everyday moments when we pay attention to these small joys. This helps us feel more positive and less stressed about the things we wish we could change.

Also, gratitude has a big impact on our mental health. Being grateful allows us to feel less depressed or anxious. This is because gratitude encourages us to think positively, which helps to push away negative thoughts. When we focus on the good, our brains release chemicals that make us feel happy and calm (that's why my favorite dessert is chocolate fudge cake—the author.)

Over time, these good feelings can help us handle tough situations better and bounce back from problems more quickly.

Another great thing about gratitude is how it improves our relationships. When we tell others that we appreciate them, it makes them feel good and strengthens our bond with them, as it did with Emma and me. As we thank them or show appreciation, it can greatly affect how close we feel to our family, friends, and coworkers. Gratitude helps build trust and respect, which are the foundations of strong relationships.

It can also make us more aware of the bigger picture. When we recognize how others have helped us, we see how interconnected we all are. This can inspire us to give back and help others in return. When we are grateful, we are more likely to be kind, generous, and supportive, creating a positive cycle that benefits everyone.

Feeling grateful isn't just good for our minds and hearts, but it is good for our bodies as well. People who practice gratitude feel fresh and activated because it reduces stress, which is harmful to our health. When we feel calm and happy, our bodies work better and stay healthier. Practicing gratitude doesn't mean ignoring the bad things in life. It is about finding balance and recognizing that, even when things are tough, there are still good things to appreciate.

This balanced view can help us feel more stable and hopeful, even in difficult times. This new perspective widened my vision of life. I recognized that being grateful makes life better. It helps us feel happier and less stressed, improves our relationships, and even boosts our health. We can enjoy life more fully by focusing on the good things, big and small. Gratitude reminds us that there is always something to be thankful for, no matter our challenges. This positive outlook can improve our lives, making each day a bit brighter and more meaningful.

Within a few minutes, just before Mom came to pick us up, Emma blew my mind. I had never thought about gratitude this way. I only thought being grateful meant saying "thank you" to someone or appreciating someone.

"Uhhh… I am tired. My feet hurt from dancing so much," I said with laughter, "But I am so grateful to you, Emma. Thank you so much for making me feel more like myself."

"You are welcome. Okay… let me tell you one more thing before we pull up," she said, "You have to be 'authentically yourself,' Claire. It is not difficult, trust me."

I looked at her and understood what she meant. Everything that I had learned through my mentorship journey with Emma broadened my perspectives.

Just before we got out of the car, we deeply discussed being authentically yourself.

Being yourself means being true to who you are, not pretending to be someone else just to fit in or make others happy. It is important to be authentically yourself because it leads to a happier, more fulfilling life. You feel more comfortable and at peace when you are true to yourself. You don't have to worry about keeping up a false image or pretending to be someone you are not. This makes life simpler and less stressful.

When you are yourself, you attract the right kind of people into your life, just like I did. Emma and I shared the most beautiful and true bond, as both of us chose to express our true selves to each other. Our friendly bond strengthened because we could be our true, authentic selves, and we always uplifted one another whenever needed, especially Emma, who stood by me when I needed it the most. She became my trusted confidant.

Therefore, we should always remember that people who like you for who you are will be drawn to you. These relationships are more genuine and satisfying because they are based on the real you. You don't have to worry about losing friends or respect if you stop pretending. The people who truly care about you will appreciate you for being authentic and accept you for who you are.

The most significant lesson of my life is that being yourself also builds self-confidence. When you accept and express your true self, you believe in your worth. You realize that you don't need to change who you are to be accepted or valued. This boosts your self-esteem and makes you feel stronger. You become more comfortable in your own skin, which helps you handle challenges and setbacks more easily.

Moreover, authenticity leads to better decision-making. When you know and accept yourself, you make choices that align with your true values and beliefs. The opinions of others or peer pressure do not influence you. This means your decisions are more likely to lead to happiness and success based on what truly matters to you.

Being true to yourself also fosters creativity and innovation. When you are not afraid to express your unique thoughts and ideas, you can come up with creative projects and original solutions. Pretending to be someone else can suppress your creativity because you are constantly trying to fit into a mold that doesn't match your true self. Embracing your authentic self allows your natural talents and ideas to flourish.

Living authentically also encourages others to do the same. When people see you being true to yourself, it inspires them to be true to themselves as well. This can create a positive environment where everyone feels free to express their real selves. It promotes honesty and openness, leading to deeper and more meaningful connections.

Moreover, being yourself brings a sense of inner peace and fulfillment. Not pretending or hiding parts of yourself makes you feel more aligned with your inner values and desires. This creates a feeling of harmony and satisfaction in life. You are more likely to feel content and happy because you are living in a way that is true to who you really are.

All in all, I learned to be authentically myself and recognized how crucial it is for a happy and fulfilling life. It reduces stress, builds self-confidence, and helps you form genuine relationships. It also brings inner peace and a deep sense of fulfillment. So, embrace who you are, with all your unique qualities and imperfections. By being true to yourself, you create a genuinely satisfying and meaningful life.

Then it was time to get out of the car. Emma and I had the best and most entertaining night together since we became friends. Also, she was going to stay over, as it was the weekend. We had planned all the activities for the night. I prepared board games, video games, our gossip session, and snacks, and was extremely excited!

"We are going to have so much fun tonight," I exclaimed, as I ran inside the house.

Emma also came rushing behind me. We rushed upstairs to my room to change into our comfy pajamas.

In between all the fun we were having, I realized what an impact good mentorship had on me. The liberation I felt within was commendable and showed in how I behaved now.

Emma and I had become best friends and looked forward to many more years of friendship together!

***

www.ingramcontent.com/pod-product-compliance
Lightning Source LLC
Chambersburg PA
CBHW061345140726
47997CB00003B/1067